A Dump Truck's Day

by Betsy Rathburn
Illustrated by Mike Byrne

BLASTOFF!
MISSIONS

BELLWETHER MEDIA
MINNEAPOLIS, MN

BLASTOFF! MISSIONS

Blastoff! Missions takes you on a learning adventure! Colorful illustrations and exciting narratives highlight cool facts about our world and beyond. Read the mission goals and follow the narrative to gain knowledge, build reading skills, and have fun!

Traditional Nonfiction

BLASTOFF! READERS

BLASTOFF! Beginners

BLASTOFF! DISCOVERY

BLASTOFF! MISSIONS

Narrative Nonfiction

Blastoff! Universe

MISSION GOALS

> FIND YOUR SIGHT WORDS IN THE BOOK.

> LEARN ABOUT HOW DUMP TRUCKS WORK IN MINES.

> THINK OF QUESTIONS TO ASK WHILE YOU READ.

This edition first published in 2023 by Bellwether Media, Inc.

Library of Congress Cataloging-in-Publication Data

Names: Rathburn, Betsy, author.
Title: A dump truck's day / by Betsy Rathburn.
Description: Minneapolis, MN : Bellwether Media, Inc., 2023. | Series: Blastoff! Missions: Machines at Work | Includes bibliographical references and index. | Audience: Ages 5-8 | Audience: Grades 2-3 |
Summary: "Vibrant illustrations accompany information about the daily tasks of a dump truck. The narrative nonfiction text is intended for students in kindergarten through third grade."-- Provided by publisher.
Identifiers: LCCN 2022013618 (print) | LCCN 2022013619 (ebook) | ISBN 9781644876626 (library binding) | ISBN 9781648348464 (paperback) | ISBN 9781648347085 (ebook)
Subjects: LCSH: Dump trucks--Juvenile literature.
Classification: LCC TL230.15 .R37 2023 (print) | LCC TL230.15 (ebook) | DDC 629.224--dc23/eng/20220411
LC record available at https://lccn.loc.gov/2022013618
LC ebook record available at https://lccn.loc.gov/2022013619

Editor: Christina Leaf   Designer: Andrea Schneider

Printed in the United States of America, North Mankato, MN.

This is **Blastoff Jimmy**! He is here to help you on your mission and share fun facts along the way!

Table of Contents

Morning at the Mine

pit mine

The sun rises over the **pit mine**. Miners are just starting to arrive. Good morning!

A dump truck waits
at the edge of the mine.
It is ready to do its job!

Other dump trucks work on **construction sites**. But this dump truck is much bigger. It works best in deep pit mines!

cab

miner

Today, the dump truck has many **loads** to carry. A miner climbs a ladder into the **cab**.

He starts the big **engine**.
A loud rumble fills the air.

The miner steers the dump truck along the rim of the mine.

treads

Its six huge tires carry
the truck down into the mine.
Deep **treads** keep the truck
steady on bumpy ground.

The dump truck heads down the **haul road**. Other dump trucks follow in a line.

It takes many trucks to do this job!

haul road

Finally, the dump truck reaches the bottom. It stops near a tall pile of rock.

excavator

dump box

An **excavator** drops scoop after scoop into the **dump box**. It is a heavy load!

Now the dump box is full. The miner drives the dump truck up the haul road again.

JIMMY SAYS

The world's biggest mining dump truck can haul more than 992,000 pounds (449,964 kilograms)!

It is a long way up! At last, it reaches the **stockyard**.

Beep! Beep! The dump truck backs up. Watch out!

The miner pulls a lever in the cab. The dump box tips back. The load falls out!

load

Empty Again

Now this job is done.
The miner steers
the dump truck
back to the bottom
of the mine.

It is time to haul
another load!

Dump Truck Jobs

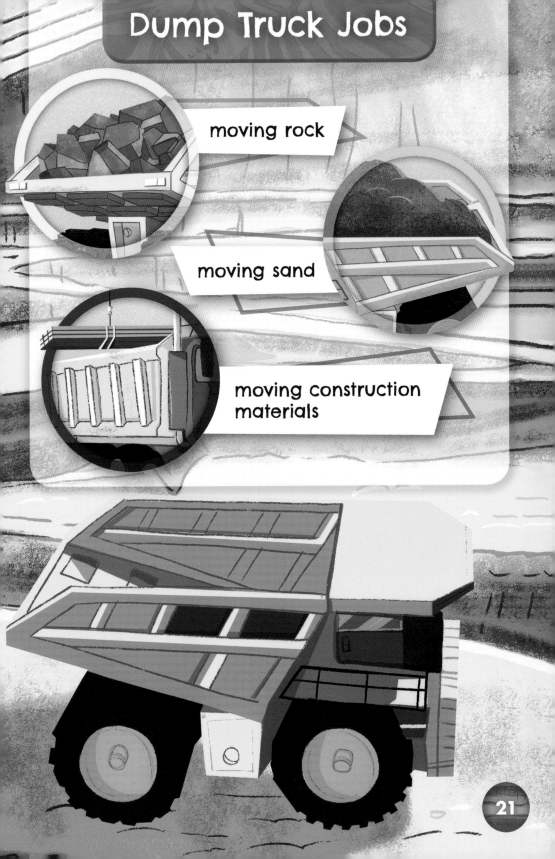

moving rock

moving sand

moving construction materials

Glossary

cab–the inside of a dump truck where the driver sits

construction sites–places where building projects are done

dump box–the part of a dump truck that carries loads

engine–the part of a dump truck that makes it go

excavator–a machine that digs

haul road–a road in a pit mine that dump trucks drive on

loads–the materials that dump trucks carry

pit mine–a place where rocks and other materials are dug up

stockyard–the place where a dump truck drops off loads

treads–deep grooves in tires that help them grip

To Learn More

AT THE LIBRARY

Allan, John. *Let's Look at Monster Machines.* Minneapolis, Minn.: Hungry Tomato, 2019.

Harasymiw, Martin. *Dump Trucks.* New York, N.Y.: Gareth Stevens Publishing, 2022.

Rogers, Marie. *Huge Earthmovers.* New York, N.Y.: PowerKids Press, 2022.

ON THE WEB

FACTSURFER

Factsurfer.com gives you a safe, fun way to find more information.

1. Go to www.factsurfer.com.

2. Enter "dump trucks" into the search box and click 🔍.

3. Select your book cover to see a list of related content.

BEYOND THE MISSION

> WHAT PART OF THE BOOK SURPRISED YOU THE MOST? WHY?

> WHAT WOULD YOU CARRY IF YOU HAD A DUMP TRUCK?

> ADD SOME FEATURES TO YOUR DUMP TRUCK. WHAT DO THEY DO?

Index